THIS
BEAUTIFUL
DAY

Also by

FRED ROGERS

The World According to Mister Rogers

Life's Journeys According to Mister Rogers

Many Ways to Say I Love You

THIS BEAUTIFUL DAY

*Daily Wisdom
from Mister Rogers*

FRED ROGERS

Introduction by LeVar Burton

hachette
BOOKS

NEW YORK

Hachette Go, an imprint of Hachette Books
Hachette Book Group
1290 Avenue of the Americas
New York, NY 10104
HachetteGo.com
Facebook.com/HachetteGo
Instagram.com/HachetteGo

First Edition: December 2024

Published by Hachette Go, an imprint of Hachette Book Group, Inc. The Hachette Go name and logo is a trademark of the Hachette Book Group.

The Hachette Speakers Bureau provides a wide range of authors for speaking events. To find out more, go to hachettespeakersbureau.com or email HachetteSpeakers@hbgusa.com.

Hachette Go books may be purchased in bulk for business, educational, or promotional use. For information, please contact your local bookseller or Hachette Book Group Special Markets Department at: special.markets@hbgusa.com.

The publisher is not responsible for websites (or their content) that are not owned by the publisher.

Print book interior design by Bart Dawson.

Library of Congress Cataloging-in-Publication Data has been applied for.

Material from this book was first published in:
The World According to Mister Rogers
The Many Ways to Say I Love You
Life's Journeys According to Mister Rogers

ISBNs: 9780306835315 (trade paperback); 9780306835322 (ebook)

Printed in the United States of America

LSC-C

Printing 1, 2024

THIS
BEAUTIFUL
DAY

INTRODUCTION
By LeVar Burton

I believe that Fred Rogers was a saint. A living, breathing saint. That is my belief. My experience of the man was that he was a bona fide bodhisattva, an enlightened being on a destiny path of the highest calling. Of course I have no proof of this. The Catholic Church, one of the world's most trusted authorities in such matters, hasn't canonized him yet. In life, Fred was a Presbyterian and an ordained minister to boot, so I'm not certain he'd even be on their saint-seeking radar if there is such a thing. I spent quite a bit of time as a Catholic myself earlier in my life—from baptism well into my twenties—and when I was around ten or eleven years old, I had an unquenchable thirst for stories about the lives of saints. I was captivated by the notion that men and women, who came from mostly humble beginnings, could somehow manage to conduct their lives in such a profound and exemplary way so as to be recognized by arguably the most powerful force in Christendom. All these years later, my takeaway from the dozens of biographies of saintly lives I read as a child is that they all seemed to have at least three traits in common. First and foremost, saints were people who possessed a core belief in a power much greater than themselves—a higher authority of a spiritual nature that was outside of worldly dominion.

Secondly, they dedicated their lives to the service of others, actively addressing themselves to the elevation of the human condition through their actions in the world. And finally, they all seemed to be driven by a boundless sense of love and compassion for humanity, notably our frailties as well as our considerable potential. Check, check, and check! Fred possessed all these qualities and more as he was simply one of the most authentic human beings I have ever encountered. He knew who he was and why he was here, and he was dedicated to a practice of sharing the best of himself, unashamedly, with the world. He exuded empathy, embodied patience and kindness, communicated in a language rooted in gratitude and grace, wonder, and reverence, so that we might by his example identify those same qualities in ourselves.

I am forever grateful to Fred for being the role model I needed when I needed one the most. We met for the first time at a PBS function in Washington, DC, during the summer of 1983 or 1984, very early on in the production of *Reading Rainbow*. I remember being eager to meet the man behind what I was convinced was a television persona he'd created in Mr. Rogers. I was sure it was an act. It became immediately clear to me that Fred was not playing a character on TV; he was showing up as his authentic self in every episode of *Mister Rogers' Neighborhood*. Fred was that present, that focused, that in the moment, with an open heart. Being in his presence that day blew my mind.

Later, as we got to know each other better, we'd have conversations about the value of engaging with an audience of children in an authentic manner. More than anyone it was Fred who encouraged me to consider my work as ministry: to connect with an audience through storytelling, bringing my authentic self to each and every moment and in that process perhaps someone in the audience might recognize a piece of their authentic self in the experience. I miss Fred. His curiosity, his compassion, his joy. His total commitment to simply being himself. May the wisdom in these pages inspire you as they have me and may the example of his life serve as inspiration for your own. It's what saints do.

THIS
BEAUTIFUL
DAY

1.

> **I would like to tell you what I often told you when you were much younger:** *I like you just the way you are.*

2.

Many adults feel that they are
falling short in one, if not all,
of the "assignments" of their lives.
They often feel they are failures.
Well, people are not failures when
they're doing the best they can. . . .
Our performance doesn't have to be
measured against anyone else's—
just against our own abilities to cope.

3.

There's the good guy and the bad guy
in all of us, but knowing that doesn't
ever need to overwhelm us.
Whatever we adults can do to help
ourselves—and anybody else—
discover that that's true can really
make a difference in this life.

4.

The world needs a sense
of *worth*, and it will achieve it
only by its people *feeling*
that they are *worthwhile*.

5.

There are many times that I wish
I had heard that "just who you
are at this moment, with the way
that you're feeling, is fine.
You don't have to be anything
more than who you are right now."
I'd like to think it's also something
that's happened to me through the
years, that I'm more able to accept
myself as I happen to be, rather than
as somebody thought I should be.

6.

Being a giver *grows* out of the experience of having been a *receiver*—a receiver who has been lovingly given to.

7.

"Each person in the world is a unique human being, and each has unique human potential. One of the important tasks of growing is the discovery of this uniqueness: the discovery of 'who I am' in each of us— of 'who I am' in relation to all those whom I meet."

8.

"Understanding love is one of the hardest things in the world."

9.

Children's play is not just kids' stuff.
Children's play is rather the
stuff of most future inventions.
Think how many people
played about going to the moon
before that was ever a reality.
Let your imagination help you to
know the truth about your identity.

10.

Our deep sense of knowing that
we are cared for is probably the most
important thing we human beings
have for coping with the perpetual
changes in our bodies, in our lives,
and in the world around us.

11.

Forgiveness is a strange thing.
It can sometimes be
easier to forgive our enemies
than our friends.

12.

People have said, "Don't cry"
to other people for years and years,
and all it has ever meant is,
"I'm too uncomfortable when
you show your feelings. Don't cry."
I'd rather have them say, "Go ahead
and cry. I'm here to be with you."

13.

If you grew up with our *Neighborhood*, you may remember how we sometimes talked about difficult things. There were days . . . even beautiful days . . . that weren't happy. In fact, there were some that were really sad.

Well, we've had a lot of days like that in our whole world. We've seen what some people do when they don't know anything else to do with their anger.

I'm convinced that when we help our children find healthy ways of dealing with their feelings—ways that don't hurt them or anyone else—we're helping to make our world a safer, better place.

14.

Since we were children once,
the roots for our empathy are
already planted within us.
We've known what it was like
to feel small and powerless,
helpless and confused.

15.

Fame is a four-letter word;
and like tape or zoom or face
or pain or life or love,
what ultimately matters
is what we *do with it*.

16.

"Anything that's human is mentionable, and anything that is mentionable can be more manageable."

17.

Feelings from childhood—
both the pleasant and
the tough—never go away.
They may get hidden,
but they're always part
of who we are.

18.

" Listening is a very active
awareness of the coming
together of at least two lives.
Listening, as far as I'm
concerned, is certainly
a prerequisite of love. "

19.

Mutually caring relationships require
kindness and patience, tolerance,
optimism, joy in the other's achievements,
confidence in oneself, and the ability
to give without undue thought of gain.
We need to accept the fact that
it's not in the power of any human being
to provide all these things all the time.
For any of us, mutually caring relationships
will also always include some measure of
unkindness and impatience, intolerance,
pessimism, envy, self-doubt,
and disappointment.

20.

Discovering the *truth* about ourselves is a lifetime's *work*, but it's *worth* the effort.

21.

We start traveling down
one street, and we find
ourselves interested in
something we never expected
on a side street; and as
we explore it, the side street
becomes the main road for us.

22.

It's very dramatic when two people
come together to work
something out. It's easy to take
a gun and annihilate your
opposition, but what is really
exciting to me is to see people with
differing views come together
and finally respect each other.

23.

"We can't be expected to leave the unhappy and angry parts of ourselves at the door before coming in. We all need to feel that we can bring the whole of ourselves to the people who care about us."

24.

The real issue in life is not
how many blessings we have,
but what we do with our
blessings. Some people
have many blessings and
hoard them. Some have few
and give everything away.

25.

"The difficult truth is that there are real limits to how much comfort we can bring to loved ones when they hurt."

26.

I don't know that I'll be alive when
my grandsons have children, and so they
just may be the last Rogerses that I'm
acquainted with on this earth.
I know they will have lots inside of
them to give to their children or nieces
or nephews. But still, it is really fun
for me to see them doing things
that I know Rogerses have done for
a long, long time. There is a
continuity that goes through the
generations. My friend and teacher,
Dr. Margaret McFarland, used to say,
"I love being part of the beach of life—
I like being one of the grains of sand."

27.

In times of stress, the best thing we can do for each other is to listen with our ears and our hearts and to be assured that our questions are just as important as our answers.

28.

What matters isn't how
a person's inner life finally puts
together the alphabet and numbers
of his outer life. What really matters
is whether he uses the alphabet for
the declaration of a war or the
description of a sunrise—his numbers
for the final count at Buchenwald
or the specifics of a brand-new bridge.

29.

Some days, doing "the best we can" may still fall short of what we would like to be able to do, but life isn't perfect—on any front—and doing what we can with what we have is the most we should expect of ourselves or anyone else.

30.

I believe that at the center of the
universe there dwells a loving spirit
who longs for all that's best in all of
creation, a spirit who knows the great
potential of each planet as well as
each person, and little by little
will love us into being more than
we ever dreamed possible.
That loving spirit would rather die
than give up on any one of us.

31.

" There's something unique
about being a member
of a family that really needs
you in order to function well.
One of the deepest longings
a person can have is to
feel needed and essential. "

32.

When I was a kid, I was shy and overweight. I was a perfect target for ridicule.

One day (how well I remember that day, and it's more than sixty years ago!) we got out of school early, and I started to walk home by myself. It wasn't long before I sensed I was being followed—by a whole group of boys. As I walked faster, I looked around, and they started to call my name and came closer and closer and got louder and louder.

"Freddy, hey, fat Freddy. We're going to get you, Freddy."

I resented those kids for not seeing beyond my fatness or my shyness. And I didn't know that it was all right to resent it, to feel bad about it, even to feel very sad about it. I didn't know it was all right to feel any of those things, because the advice I got from the grown-ups was, "Just let on you don't care, then nobody will bother you."

What I actually did was mourn. I cried to myself whenever I was alone. I cried through my fingers as I made up songs on the piano. I sought out stories of other people who were poor in spirit, and I felt for them. . . .

"Let on you don't care, then nobody will bother you." Those who gave me that advice were well-meaning people; but, of course, I did care, and somehow along the way I caught the belief that God cares, too; that the divine presence cares for those of us who are hurting and that presence is everywhere. I don't know exactly how this came to me, maybe through one of my teachers or the town librarian, maybe through a musician or a minister—definitely across some holy ground. And, of course, it could have come from the grandfather I was named for: Fred McFeely, who used to say to me after we'd had a visit together, "Freddy, you made this day a special day for me."

33.

From the very beginning of our lives,
we've had a natural need to receive.
Without it, we couldn't have grown.
We wouldn't have wanted nourishment;
we wouldn't have wanted care.
And what we must realize is that we
do not outgrow this need to receive.
Receiving times are for everybody,
and so are giving times.

34.

I hope you will feel *good*
enough about yourselves
that you will want to *minister*
to others, and that you
will find your own *unique*
ways to do that.

35.

I realize that it isn't very fashionable
to talk about some things as
being holy; nevertheless, if we ever
want to rid ourselves of personal
and corporate emptiness, brokenness,
loneliness, and fear, we will have
to allow ourselves room for that
which we cannot see, hear,
touch, or control.

36.

I'm *proud* of you for times
you wrestled with your
problems and *discovered*
how much that helped
you to *grow*.

37.

It takes strength to acknowledge
our anger, and sometimes more
strength yet to curb the aggressive
urges anger may bring and to
channel them into nonviolent
outlets. It takes strength to face
our sadness and to grieve and to
let our grief and our anger flow
in tears when they need to.
It takes strength to talk about
our feelings and to reach out for
help and comfort when we need it.

38.

"It's the things we play with and the people who help us play that make a great difference in our lives."

39.

One of the *strongest* things
we have to wrestle with in our lives
is the significance of the *longing*
for *perfection* in ourselves and in
the people bound to us by *friendship*
or *parenthood* or *childhood*.

40.

What makes the *difference* between
wishing and *realizing* our wishes?
Lots of things, and it may take months
or years for a wish to come true,
but it's far more likely to happen when
you *care* so much about a wish that
you'll do all you can to make it *happen*.

41.

The older I get, the more I seem
to be able to appreciate my "neighbor"
(whomever I happen to be with at
the moment). Oh, sure, I've always
tried to love my neighbor as myself;
however, the more experiences I've
had, the more chances I've had to see
the uniqueness of each person . . . as
well as each tree, and plant, and shell,
and cloud . . . the more I find myself
delighting every day in the lavish gifts
of God, whom I've come to believe is
the greatest appreciator of all.

42.

"Each one of us contributes
in some unique way to
the composition of life."

43.

But how do we make *goodness* attractive?
By doing whatever we can do to bring
courage to those whose lives move
near our own—by *treating* our
"neighbor" at least as well as we
treat ourselves and *allowing* that
to inform everything we produce.

44.

If we're really honest with ourselves,
there are probably times when we think,
"What possible use can I be in
this world? What need is there for
somebody like me to fill?"
That's one of the deeper mysteries.
Then God's grace comes to us
in the form of another person who
tells us we have been of help,
and what a blessing that is.

45.

It's no secret that I like to
get to *know* people—
and not just the outside stuff
of their lives. I like to try to
understand the *meaning*
of *who* people are and *what*
they're saying to me.

46.

From the song
The Truth Will Make Me Free

What if I were very, very sad
And all I did was smile?
I wonder after awhile
What might become of my sadness?
What if I were very very angry?
And all I did was sit
And never think about it?
What might become of my anger?
Where would they go?
And what would they do,
If I couldn't let them out?
Maybe I'd fall, maybe get sick
Or doubt.
But what if I could know the truth
And say just how I feel?
I think I'd learn a lot that's real
About freedom.

47.

"The greatest gift
you ever give is
your honest self."

48.

If I'm sad about something, and I dismiss my sadness by saying, "Oh, well, it was for the best," then I'm probably not willing or able to explore how I'm feeling. If I'm angry with someone, and I say, "Oh, it doesn't matter, I don't care," then I probably don't know what I'm really feeling.

On the other hand, if we can allow ourselves to be gentle with ourselves no matter what our feelings may be, we have the chance of discovering the very deep roots of who we are.

49.

Understanding invariably
leads to finding
caring ways to help.

50.

The greatest *loss* that
we all have to deal with
is the loss of the
image of ourselves as
a *perfect* person.

51.

Music is the one art we all have inside.
We may not be able to play an instrument,
but we can sing along or clap
or tap our feet. Have you ever seen
a baby bouncing up and down
in the crib in time to some music?
When you think of it, some of that
baby's first messages from his or her
parents may have been lullabies, or at least
the music of their speaking voices.
All of us have had the experience of
hearing a tune from childhood
and having that melody evoke
a memory or a feeling.
The music we hear early on tends
to stay with us all our lives.

52.

Do your best to *appreciate*
the gifts that you really are
and always will be . . . to look
for every *opportunity* that
allows you to clap and cheer,
loving your neighbor as yourself.

53.

Please think of the children first.
If you ever have anything to do
with their entertainment,
their food, their toys, their custody,
their day or night care,
their health care, their education—
listen to the children, learn
about them, learn from them.
Think of the children first.

54.

My personal introduction to the Dalai Lama was by way of television—in a hotel room. I was in Washington, D.C., preparing for a conference on children and the media and was looking for a certain news program when I happened upon His Holiness saying, "Someone else's action should not determine your response." I was so intrigued, I wrote down those words, turned off the television, and thought about nothing else the whole evening.

"Someone else's action should not determine your response." It sounds so simple, doesn't it? And yet what if someone else's action should be shouting angry words at us or hitting us with a rotten tomato? That doesn't affect what we do in response? Not if our compassion is genuine. Not if our love is the kind the Dalai Lama advocates.

55.

From the song
I'm Still Myself Inside

I can put on a hat, or put on a coat,
Or wear a pair of glasses or sail in a boat.
I can change all my names and find a place
to hide.
I can do almost anything, but I'm still
myself inside.
I can go far away, or dream anything,
Or wear a scary costume or act like a king.
I can change all my names and find a place
to hide.
I can do almost anything, but I'm still
myself,
I'm still myself,
I'm still myself inside.

56.

"Who you are inside
is what helps you
make and do
everything in life."

57.

A high school student wrote to ask, "What was the greatest event in American history?" I can't say. However, I suspect that like so many "great" events, it was something very simple and very quiet with little or no fanfare (such as someone forgiving someone else for a deep hurt that eventually changed the course of history).

58.

It's true that we take a great deal
of our own upbringing on into
our adult lives and our lives as
parents; but it's true, too, that
we can change some of the things
that we would like to change.
It can be hard, but it can be done.

59.

Actor David Carradine, son of
John Carradine, said in gratitude
of his father's accomplishments,
"I could stand on his shoulders
and feel twice as tall."
That each generation could
stand on the shoulders of the last
and feel twice as tall is a
poetic hope for all our families.

60.

Part of the problem with the word
disabilities is that it immediately
suggests an inability to see or hear
or walk or do other things that many of us
take for granted. But what of people who
can't feel? Or talk about their feelings?
Or manage their feelings in
constructive ways? What of people
who aren't able to form close and
strong relationships? And people who
cannot find fulfillment in their lives,
or those who have lost hope, who live
in disappointment and bitterness and find
in life no joy, no love? These, it seems to
me, are the real disabilities.

61.

You are a very special person.
There is only one like you
in the whole world.
There's never been anyone
exactly like you before,
and there never will be again.
Only you. And people can
like you exactly as you are.

62.

It's not always easy for a father
to understand the interests
and ways of his son.
It seems the songs of our
children may be in keys
we've never tried. The melody
of each generation emerges
from all that's gone before.

63.

I think the young feel pressured by
the older generation. But I realized it
isn't just the older generation doing
the pressuring. Young people are
pressuring older people to change, too,
and it can make us feel uncomfortable.
But it isn't all bad either. I know how much
I learned from my parents and teachers,
and now I know for sure that I'm learning
from my children and the young people
I work with. I don't do everything
they want me to do, and they don't do
everything I want them to do, but we know
down deep we'd really be impoverished
if we didn't have each other.

64.

"It can be hardest of all to forgive people we love. Like all of life's important coping skills, the ability to forgive and the capacity to let go of resentments most likely take root very early in our lives."

65.

Yo-Yo Ma is one of the most other-oriented geniuses I've ever known. His music comes from a place very deep within his being. During a master class, Yo-Yo gently led young cellists into understandings about their instruments, their music, and their "selves," which, some of them told me later, they would carry with them forever.

I can still see the face of one young man who had just finished playing a movement of a Brahms cello sonata when Yo-Yo said, "Nobody else can make the sound you make." Of course, he meant it as a compliment to the young man; nevertheless, he meant that also for everyone in the class. Nobody else can make the sound you make. Nobody can choose to make that particular sound in that particular way.

66.

All of us, at some time or other, need help. Whether we're giving or receiving help, each one of us has something valuable to bring to this world. That's one of the things that connects us as neighbors—in our own way, each one of us is a giver and a receiver.

67.

We all have different *gifts*,
so we all have different ways
of saying to the world
who we are.

68.

When we can resign ourselves to
the wishes that will never come true,
there can be enormous energies
available within us for whatever we
can do. I know a woman who
remembers the time when her wish
to have children would not be realized.
She remembers the struggle of the final
resignation, and then she remembers
the outcome of that resignation.
Enormous energies were available to her,
which she used in developing uniquely
creative work with young parents.

69.

We all long to be cared for,
and that longing lies at
the root of our ability
to be caregivers.

70.

I wish you the kind of life's
work in which you can use
the greatest part of who
you are; and I wish you the
kind of life's love that will
enhance all that you do,
as well as all that you are.

71.

"When we can talk about our feelings, they become less overwhelming, less upsetting, and less scary. The people we trust with that important talk can help us know that we're not alone."

72.

What's been important in my
understanding of myself and others
is the fact that each one of us is
so much more than any one thing.
A sick child is much more than his or
her sickness. A person with a disability
is much, much more than a handicap.
A pediatrician is more than a medical
doctor. You're much more than your
job description or your age or
your income or your output.

73.

Isn't it *amazing* how much
we bring of *who* we've been
to whatever we do *today*!
And that happens
all through *life*.

74.

From the song
It's You I Like

It's you I like,
It's not the things you wear.
It's not the way you do your hair.
But it's you I like.
The way you are right now,
The way down deep inside you,
Not the things that hide you,
Not your toys, they're just beside you.
But it's you I like, every part of you,
Your skin, your eyes, your feelings
Whether old or new.
I hope that you'll remember
Even when you're feeling blue
That it's you I like,
It's your yourself, it's you,
It's you . . . I . . . like!

75.

It's not the honors and the prizes
and the fancy outsides of life
that ultimately nourish our souls.
It's the knowing that we can
be trusted, that we never have
to fear the truth, that the bedrock
of our very being is firm.

76.

Often out of periods of losing come the greatest strivings toward a new winning streak.

77.

There's a part of all of us
that *longs* to know
that even what's weakest
about us is still *redeemable*
and can ultimately count
for something *good*.

78.

My own friend and companion, when I was little and didn't yet have a sister, was Mitzi, a brown, wire-haired mongrel. We played and had long "conversations" during which she heard many of my secrets and shared my joys and sadnesses. We ran in the fields and huddled together through thunderstorms. I gave a great deal of myself to Mitzi, and she faithfully reflected that self back to me, helping me learn more about who I was and, in those early days, what I was feeling. When she died, she went on teaching me—about loss and grief . . . and about the renewal of hope and joy.

79.

One of my mentors, Dr. C., worked with us every week for thirty years. He listened to ideas for scripts and songs and toys and books and records and speeches; and, over that time, he helped all of us who consulted with him realize that somehow we were uniquely suited for what we were doing.

Through those years, each one of us in our particular neighborhood grew at our own pace along the road of maturity both professionally and personally. Dr. C. had that innate gift in everything that he said and did, which allowed people who worked with him to develop from within.

As I think back on those thirty years of work with Dr. C., I realize anew that he never hurried us. We were never made to feel that we had to be somebody that we were not, yet we were always encouraged to choose to be the best of who we were at the moment. Indeed, our development was far from overnight—we become who we are over time.

80.

When you combine your own
intuition with a sensitivity
to other people's feelings and moods,
you may be close to the origins of
valuable human attributes such
as generosity, altruism, compassion,
sympathy, and empathy.

81.

"Shyness isn't something that just children feel. Anybody can feel shy. And one reason we feel that way is that we're not sure people will like us just the way we are."

82.

There's no "should" or "should not"
when it comes to having feelings.
They're part of who we are and their
origins are beyond our control.
When we can believe that,
we may find it easier to make
constructive choices about
what to do with those feelings.

83.

Nobody else can live the life
you live. And even though
no human being is perfect,
we always have the chance
to bring what's unique
about us to life.

84.

Whatever we choose
to imagine can be as
private as we want it to be.
Nobody knows what
you're thinking or feeling
unless you share it.

85.

A young apprentice applied to a
master carpenter for a job. The older
man asked him, "Do you know
your trade?" "Yes, sir!" the young man
replied proudly. "Have you ever made
a mistake?" the older man inquired.
"No, sir!" the young man answered,
feeling certain he would get the job.
"Then there's no way I'm going to
hire you," said the master carpenter,
"because when you make one,
you won't know how to fix it."

86.

One of my seminary professors, Dr. Orr, often talked with great poignancy about Henry, a student who had come to the seminary with a degree in classic literature and a fine working knowledge of Greek and Latin as well as several modern languages. He remembered this young man as being brilliant and yet always receiving with such grace the offers of others.

It seems that this young man was a perfectionist. For him every word had to be just so. Even though he tried hard, it became clear to him that he was not going to be suited for the parish ministry. Eventually, he dropped out of seminary and took a job at a local department store.

Dr. Orr didn't hear from him for a long while, so one day, he stopped in the store to see how Henry was faring. It happened to be Henry's day off, but his coworkers talked with Dr. Orr about him. The more they talked, the more Dr. Orr realized that the people at the store knew nothing about this fellow employee's extensive education. What they did know was what had happened in their department after his arrival. "This department was filled with all kinds of jealousy and pettiness. It was a miserable place to work before Henry came," a person told Dr. Orr. "But after he had been here awhile, somehow all of that miserable stuff seemed to disappear. We all got working together, and well, it's different with him here. He is like a minister in more ways than anyone ever knows. You say you know Henry? Well, you are blessed, too, then."

Dr. Orr finally contacted Henry, and the two of them read Greek literature together for ten years before Henry died. When Dr. Orr talked about him, he would invariably say, "To think there were people at the seminary—and elsewhere—who called it a waste for Henry to have done what he did, working at that department store." Then Dr. Orr would add, "Henry probably had one of the greatest ministries I know. I feel privileged to have been his friend."

87.

It seems to me that the most essential
element in the development of
any creation must be love—a love that
begins in the simple expressions of care
for a little child, and, once received,
goes on to mature into responsible
feelings about ourselves and others.

88.

We'd all like to feel self-reliant
and capable of coping with whatever
adversity comes our way, but that's
not how most human beings are made.
It's my belief that the capacity to
accept help is inseparable from
the capacity to give help when
our turn comes to be strong.

89.

I wonder if we might pledge ourselves
to remember what life is really
all about—not to be afraid that we're
less flashy than the next, not to
worry that our influence is not that
of a tornado, but rather that of
a grain of sand in an oyster!
Do we have that kind of patience?

90.

Listening is where
love begins:
listening to *ourselves*
and then to our *neighbors*.

91.

" It's really easy to fall into
the trap of believing that
what we do is more important
than what we are. Of course,
it's the opposite that's true:
What we are ultimately
determines what we do! "

92.

I remember when my mentor Dr. Margaret McFarland said, "You know, Fred, in everyone's life there are times for looking back at who we've been and what we've done, times for remembering who cheered us when we were sad, who held us when we were mad, who laughed with us when we were happy."

I wonder what you may have in your personal history that has been a comfort to you? Reach inside yourself and try to remember what someone you loved said to you or did for you when you needed comfort as a child.

93.

There's a *nurturing* element
to all human beings,
whenever they themselves
have *been* nurtured,
and it's going to be *expressed*
one way or another.

94.

My grandfather was one of those people
who loved to live and loved to teach.
Every time I was with him, he'd show me
something about the world or something
about myself that I hadn't even thought
of yet. He'd help me find something
wonderful in the smallest of things,
and ever so carefully, he helped me
understand the enormous worth of every
human being. My grandfather was not
a professional teacher, but the way
he treated me (the way he loved me)
and the things he did with me, served me
as well as any teacher I've ever known.

95.

When I was a boy, one of my closest neighbors was Mama Bell Frampton. She was my grandmother's age, and she loved children. She not only had a front porch, she had a back porch that led right to her kitchen. Every time I needed a treat, I'd knock on her back door and she'd welcome me. "Come for toast sticks, Freddy?" She knew me well.

I would have been about five or six when Mama Bell asked if I would like her to show me how to make my own toast sticks. Well, that was quite a day. She let me put the bread in the toaster and the butter and jam on the toast, and she even let me (ever so carefully) cut the toast into four long "sticks." Seems like a simple thing, but sixty-five years later, I can still feel it—that neighbor's trust and my own pride at having made those first ones on my own. When I hear "Love your neighbor as yourself," I often think of Mama Bell because I think she really did love me. She just somehow sensed what I needed in order to grow.

96.

One of the greatest paradoxes
about omnipotence is that
we need to feel it early in life,
and lose it early in life,
in order to achieve a healthy,
realistic, yet exciting,
sense of potency later on.

97.

When people help us to feel
good about who we are,
they are really helping us to
love the meaning of what
we *create* in this life.

98.

The gifts we treasure most over
the years are often small and simple.
In easy times and in tough times,
what seems to matter most
is the way we show those
nearest us that we've been
listening to their needs, to their
joys, and to their challenges.

99.

I need thinking time when someone
asks me a searching question.
I wonder why it seems to be so
uncomfortable for many people
to wait through the silence.
People of all ages have deep feelings,
and if we have the patience to
wait through the silence, it's often
astounding what people will tell us.

100.

"Learning and *loving*
go hand in hand."*

101.

Here's a gift you may not have expected.
It's a gift for you to give yourself.
Sometime in your day today,
try to turn off all the noises you can
around you, and give yourself
some "quiet time." In the silence,
let yourself think about
something. Or if possible . . .
think about nothing.

102.

Development comes
from within.
Nature does not hurry
but advances slowly.

103.

Music has given me a way of expressing
my feelings and my thoughts,
and it has also given me a way of
understanding more about life.
For example, as you play together in
a symphony orchestra, you can
appreciate that each musician has
something fine to offer. Each one is
different, though, and you each have
a different "song to sing." When you
sing together, you make one voice.
That's true of all endeavors,
not just musical ones.

104.

"All our lives, we rework the
things from our childhood,
like feeling good about ourselves,
managing our angry feelings,
being able to say good-bye
to people we love."

105.

I can see how all the interests I had
as I was growing up served me well
in the work I finally chose to do—
writing songs, making puppets talk,
thinking up stories, looking for
helpers. It's very important, no matter
what you may do professionally,
to keep alive some of the
healthy interests of your youth.

106.

There is no normal life that is *free* of pain. It's the very wrestling with our *problems* that can be the impetus for our *growth*.

107.

Our biological makeup at birth has
much to do with who we become,
but so do our environment
and our psychological development
from one stage to another.
And how we grow with all our
unique endowments will influence
how people will respond to us.

108.

If the day ever came when we were able
to accept ourselves and our children
exactly as we and they are, then,
I believe, we would have come very
close to an ultimate understanding
of what "good" parenting means.
It's part of being human to fall short of
that total acceptance—and often far
short. But one of the most important
gifts a parent can give a child is the gift
of accepting that child's uniqueness.

109.

A few years ago I was asked to be part of a White House meeting about children and television. Many broadcasters from all over the country were there. During my speech, I asked the audience to spend one minute thinking of someone who'd made a difference in the person they'd become. As I was leaving that enormous room, I heard something from one of the military guards who was all dressed up in white and gold, looking like a statue. I heard him whisper, "Thanks, Mister Rogers."

So I went over to him and noticed his eyes were moist, and he said, "Well, sir, as I listened to you today, I started to remember my grandfather's brother. I haven't thought about him in years. I was only seven when he died, but just before that, he gave me his favorite fishing rod. I've just been thinking, maybe that's why I like fishing so much and why I like to show the kids in my neighborhood all about it."

Well, as far as I'm concerned, the major reason for my going to Washington that day was that military guard and nourishing the memory of his great-uncle. What marvelous mysteries we're privileged to be part of! Why would that young man be assigned to guard that particular room on that particular day? Slender threads like that weave this complex fabric of our life together.

110.

Solitude is *different* from loneliness, and it doesn't have to be a *lonely* kind of thing.

111.

Your history is *who* you are, and there never *has* been— and never *will* be, in the history of the earth—another person exactly like *you*.

112.

Peace means far more
than the opposite of war!

113.

How many times have you noticed
that it's the little quiet moments
in the midst of life that seem to give
the rest extra-special meaning?

114.

Imagine what our real
neighborhoods would be like
if each of us *offered,*
as a matter of course,
just one *kind* word
to another person.

115.

When my mother or my grandmother
tried to keep me from climbing
too high, my grandfather would say,
"Let the kid walk on the wall.
He's got to learn to do things for
himself." I loved my grandfather
for trusting me so much.
His name was Fred McFeely.
No wonder I included a lively,
elderly delivery man in our
television "neighborhood" whom
we named "Mr. McFeely."

116.

I received a letter from a parent who wrote: "Mister Rogers, how do you do it? I wish I were like you. I want to be patient and quiet and even-tempered, and always speak respectfully to my children. But that just isn't my personality. I often lose my patience and even scream at my children. I want to change from an impatient person into a patient person, from an angry person into a gentle one."

Just as it takes time for children to understand what real love is, it takes time for parents to understand that being always patient, quiet, even-tempered, and respectful isn't necessarily what "good" parents are. In fact, parents help children by expressing a wide range of feelings—including appropriate anger. All children need to see that the adults in their lives can feel anger and not hurt themselves or anyone else when they feel that way.

As parents, we need to try to find the security within ourselves to accept the fact that children and parents won't always like each other's actions, that there will be times when parents and children won't be able to be friends, and that there will be times of real anger in families. But we need to know, at the same time, that moments of conflict have nothing to do with whether parents and children really love one another. It's our continuing love for our children that makes us want them to become all they can be, capable of making sound choices.

117.

"Who we are in the present includes who we were in the past."

118.

There have been so many stories
about the lack of courtesy,
the impatience of today's world,
road rage and even restaurant rage.
Sometimes, all it takes is
one kind word to nourish
another person.

119.

In order to express our sense of reality, we must use some kind of symbol: words or notes or shades of paint or television pictures or sculpted forms. None of those symbols or images can ever completely satisfy us because they can never be any more than what they are—a fragment of a reflection of what we feel reality to be.

120.

I have long believed that the way to
know a spiritual sense is to know it
in our real life. I think the
best way to understand about
God and peace is to know about
peace in our everyday lives.

121.

I've often hesitated in beginning
a project because I've thought,
"It'll never turn out to be even
remotely like the good idea I have
as I start." I could just "feel" how
good it could be. But I decided that,
for the present, I would create
the best way I know how
and accept the ambiguities.

122.

Letting go is seldom easy—whether it's letting go of our children, our parents, or our childhood feelings. But just as the root systems of plants often have to be divided for healthy growth to continue, the different generations within a family may have to pull apart for a while for each to find its own healthy identity.

123.

Our parents gave us what they were
able to give, and we took what we could
of it and made it part of ourselves.
If we knew our grandparents,
and even great-grandparents,
we will have taken from them what
they could offer us, too. All that
helped to make us who we are.
We, in our turn, will offer what
we can of ourselves to our children
and their offspring.

124.

Being creative is part of being human. Everyone is creative. Each person's creativity finds different form, that's true; but without creativity of some kind, I doubt that we'd get through many of the problems that life poses.

125.

Years ago, a friend gave me a piece of calligraphy which I have always kept in my office. It's a quotation from *The Little Prince* by Antoine de Saint-Exupéry that reads, "*L'essentiel est invisible pour les yeux.*" What is essential is invisible to the eyes.

What is essential about *you* that is invisible to the eye? What are some of the things about your very being that allow you to look to the years ahead with confidence?

126.

One of our chief *jobs* in life,
it seems to me, is to realize how
rare and *valuable* each one of
us really is—that each of us has
something which no one else has—
or ever will have—something inside
which is *unique* to all time.

127.

You rarely have time for
everything you want in this life,
so you need to make choices.
And hopefully your choices
can come from a deep sense
of who you are.

128.

Erik Erikson, a psychologist whose insight into human development has been an important foundation of our work here in the Neighborhood, said that "tradition is to human beings what instinct is to animals." Imagine the chaos if animals lost their instincts. So would it be if human beings were to lose all their traditions. The study of history helps keep traditions alive.

129.

There's a world of difference
between insisting on
someone's doing something
and establishing an
atmosphere in which
that person can grow into
wanting to do it.

130.

"The outside is never as much as the inside. . . ." As you may know by now, that's one of the major themes of our work: The invisible essential. Oh, the outsides of life are important, but the insides are what enhance so much of the rest.

131.

When I graduated from college, I had little notion of how I'd ever be able to put together all the interests that I had. It took a good deal of time, and my parents probably wondered if I'd ever be able to make anything of myself.

But I'll never forget the sense of wholeness I felt when I finally realized, after a lot of help from a lot of people, what, in fact, I really was. I was not just a songwriter or a language buff or a student of human development or a telecommunicator, but someone who could use every talent that had ever been given to me in the service of children (and their families).

I can tell you that it was that particular focus that made all the difference for me. I can also tell you that the directions weren't written on the back of my college diploma. They came ever so slowly for me; and ever so firmly, I trusted that they would emerge.

132.

"It's our job to encourage each other to discover our uniqueness and to provide ways of developing its expression."

133.

Who in your life has been such a servant to you . . . who has helped you love the good that grows within you? Let's just take ten seconds to think of some of those people who have loved us and wanted what was best for us in life—those who have encouraged us to become who we are tonight—just ten seconds of silence.

No matter where they are—either here or in heaven—imagine how pleased those people must be to know that you thought of them right now.

134.

One of life's *greatest* joys
is the comfortable give-and-take
of a good *friendship*.
It's a wonderful feeling not only
to have a good friend,
but to know how
to be a good *friend*.

135.

Are you able to believe in a loving presence who desires the best for you and the whole universe?

With all the sadness and destruction, negativity and rage expressed throughout the world, it's tough not to wonder where the loving presence is. Well, we don't have to look very far. Deep within each of us is a spark of the divine just waiting to be used to light up a dark place. The only thing is—we have the free choice of using it or not. That's part of the mysterious truth of who we human beings are.

136.

Finding ways to harmonize
our uniqueness with
the uniqueness of others
can be the most fun—and
the most rewarding—of all.

137.

I have always called
talking about feelings
"important talk."
Knowing that our feelings
are natural and normal
for all of us can make it
easier for us to share them
with one another.

138.

We have all been children and have had
children's feelings, but many of us
have forgotten. We've forgotten
what it's like not to be able to reach
the light switch. We've forgotten
a lot of the monsters that seemed
to live in our room at night.
Nevertheless, those memories are
still there, somewhere inside us.

139.

But feeling good about who we are
doesn't come just from people telling us
they like us. It comes from inside of us:
knowing when we've done something
helpful or when we've worked hard to
learn something difficult or when we've
"stopped" just when we were about to
do something we shouldn't, or when
we've been especially kind to someone
else. Along with the times we're
feeling good about who we are, we can
experience times when we're feeling
bad about who we are. That's just
a part of being human.

140.

When I was young (about eight or ten
years old), I was trying to learn
so many things all at once, things like
the piano and organ and algebra and
cooking and typing, and I even started
to take clarinet lessons. But I just didn't
practice the clarinet, so I didn't learn.
I think I wanted to learn by magic.
I think that I had the idea that if I got
the clarinet I would somehow know
how to play it. But magic doesn't work
with learning, not with anything
really worthwhile.

141.

"We all make mistakes as we grow, and not only is there nothing wrong with that, there's everything right about it."

142.

All I can say is, it's worth the struggle
to discover who you really are
and how you, in your own way,
can put life together as something
that means a lot to you. It's a miracle
when you finally discover whom
you're best equipped to serve—and
we're all equipped to serve in some way.

143.

The *opposite* of love is not hate,

it's *indifference*.

I once heard a little boy

say to someone,

"You can't make me mad.

I don't even like you."

144.

I think the most important part
about communicating is the
listening we do beforehand.
When we can truly respect
what someone brings to what
we're offering, it makes
the communication all the
more meaningful.

145.

Think of the ripple effect
that can be created when
we nourish someone.
One kind empathetic word
has a wonderful way of
turning into many.

146.

What are some of the ways of showing
and telling who you are and how you're
feeling? They may be sports
or homemaking or art or music
or crafts or science or math or dance
or selling or public speaking.
Whatever they may be, and if you
know they're healthy, try to keep
embracing them, love them,
give them room to grow inside
yourself, because those gifts of
expression are so unique to you.

147.

"Children aren't the only ones
who hunger for individual
attention. Friends need
time alone together;
so do husbands and wives;
so do older parents
and their grown children."

148.

I wonder what memories of yours
will persist as you go on in life.
My hunch is that the most important
will have to do with feelings of
loving and being loved—family,
friends, teachers, shopkeepers—
whoever's been close to you.

149.

It's a *mistake* to think
that we have to be *lovely*
to be *loved* by human
beings or by God.

150.

It can be very hard to trust our own judgments when our feelings seem to be different from those of most other people. The best kind of friends are those who remind us that we are the ones who know the most about ourselves.

151.

How we deal with the big
disappointments in life depends
a great deal on how the people
who loved us helped us deal
with smaller disappointments
when we were little.

152.

If we grow up fearing mistakes,
we may become afraid to try
new things. Making mistakes is
a natural part of being human and
a natural part of the way we learn.
It's an important lesson, at any
time of life, but certainly
the earlier the better.

153.

As you continue to *grow*,
you'll find many ways of
expressing your love and you'll
discover more and more ways
in which others express
their *love* for you.

154.

From the song
There Are Many Ways to Say I Love You

There are many ways to say I love you.
There are many ways to say I care about you.
Many ways, many ways,
Many ways to say I love you.
There's the singing way to say I love you.
There's the singing something someone really likes
    to hear.
The singing way, the singing way,
The singing way to say I love you.
Cleaning up a room can say I love you.
Hanging up a coat before you're asked to.
Drawing special pictures for the holidays
And making plays.
You'll find many ways to say I love you.
You'll find many ways to understand what love is.
Many ways, many ways,
Many ways to say I love you.
Singing, cleaning, drawing, being understanding,
Love you.

155.

"Sometimes I just go over to the piano and play out my feelings through music. That kind of break seems to nourish me, and I can come back renewed."

156.

Above all, I think that the willingness
and the courage to keep on trying develops
best if there is someone we love close by
who can lend us some of the strength
we do not yet have within ourselves.
I don't mean someone who will do
a task for us, but rather someone who
will share our times of trying just by
being around and being supportive,
someone who can sustain the belief
that we can succeed even when
we doubt it ourselves. We all need
quiet, caring cheerleaders like that—
grown-ups as well as children.

157.

How great it is when we come to
know that times of disappointment
can be followed by times of fulfillment;
that sorrow can be followed by joy;
that guilt over falling short of our
ideals can be replaced by pride in
doing all that we can; and that
anger can be channeled into creative
achievements . . . and into dreams
that we can make come true!

158.

It always *helps* to have people we love *beside* us when we have to do *difficult* things in life.

159.

One of the mysteries is that as
unlike as we are, one human being
from another, we also share much
in common. Our lives begin
the same way, by birth. . . .
Yet no two threads—no two lives—
in that vast tapestry of existence have
ever been, or ever will be, the same.

160.

Anyone who has ever
been able to sustain good
work has had at least
one person—and often
many—who have believed
in him or her.

161.

We just don't get to be
competent human beings
without a lot of different
investments from others.

162.

I've had lots of heroes—lots of people I've wanted to be like. To this day, I can still feel the excitement in 1944 as I opened the first installment of my Charles Atlas exercise course. I had saved my money ($19.00) and had sent away for those lessons that I thought would help me look like Atlas himself holding up the world. In 1944, I was a chubby and weak sixteen-year-old, and Charles Atlas was trim and strong. I did the exercises every morning—some of them even had me hanging on a bar at a doorjamb. Many months and many lessons later, I still didn't look like Charles Atlas. Now, happily, I don't need to.

Maybe it's natural, especially when we're little and feel weak, to choose "outside" kinds of heroes and superheroes who can keep us safe in a scary world.

163.

For a long time, I've wondered why I felt like bowing when people showed their appreciation for the work that I've been privileged to do. It's been a kind of natural response to a feeling of great gratitude. What I've come to understand is that we who bow are probably—whether we know it or not—acknowledging the presence of the sacred. We're bowing to the sacred in our neighbor. . . .

As I bow, I always feel like saying, "Thank you, thank you, thank you."

164.

It may be easier for us if, as children,
we were allowed to have our angry
feelings and if someone we loved let us
know that those feelings were a normal
part of loving and being loved.
It will certainly have helped us if we
learned to talk about those feelings
and express them in healthy ways.

165.

"Grandparents are both our past and our future. In some ways they are what has gone before, and in others they are what we will become."

166.

My own wish for children is that
they learn to find joy even amidst the
world's and their own imperfections . . .
that they grow to have a clear
but forgiving interior voice to guide
them . . . and that they come to have
a reasonable sense of shame without
an unreasonable burden of guilt.

167.

You see, I believe that appreciation
is a holy thing—that when we look
for what's best in a person we happen
to be with at the moment, we're doing
what God does all the time.

168.

As a relationship matures, you start
to see that just being there for each
other is the most important thing
you can do, just being there to
listen and be sorry with them,
to be happy with them, to share
all that there is to share.

169.

Whether we're children or adults,
adding to our emotional vocabulary
can often add to our ability to
cope with what we're feeling.
Using words to describe what's
inside helps remind us that what
we're experiencing is human . . .
and mentioning our feelings
to others can make those
feelings more manageable.

170.

From the song
You've Got to Do It

You can make believe it happens,
Or pretend that something's true.
You can wish or hope or contemplate
A thing you'd like to do.
But until you start to do it,
You will never it through
'Cause the make-believe pretending
Just won't do it for you.
You've got to do it. Every little bit,
You've got to do it, do it, do it.
And when you're through,
You can know who did it,
For you did it, you did it, you did it.
It's not easy to keep trying,
But it's one good way to grow.
It's not easy to keep learning
But I know that this is so:
When you've tried and learned,
You're bigger than you were a day ago.
It's not easy to keep trying,
But it's one way to grow.

171.

The best gifts are often wrapped in the most unspectacular ways.

You've probably had many fancy wrapped-up gifts—gifts which dazzle the eyes and impress the neighbors; nevertheless, isn't it the "heart surprise" that lingers in your memory and serves to nourish you from year to year?

172.

From the song
When the Day Turns into Night

When the day turns into night,
And you're way beyond my sight,
I think of you, I think of you.
When the night turns into day,
And you still are far away,
I think of you, I think of you.
Even when I am not here,
We still can be so very near.
I want you to know, my dear,
I think of you.

173.

There was a story going around about the Special Olympics. For the hundred-yard dash, there were nine contestants, all of them so-called physically or mentally disabled. All nine of them assembled at the starting line and, at the sound of the gun, they took off. But one little boy didn't get very far. He stumbled and fell and hurt his knee and began to cry.

The other eight children heard the boy crying. They slowed down, turned around, and ran back to him—every one of them ran back to him. The little boy got up, and he and the rest of the runners linked their arms together and joyfully walked to the finish line.

They all finished the race at the same time. And when they did, everyone in the stadium stood up and clapped and whistled and cheered for a long, long time. And you know why? Because deep down we know that what matters in this life is more than winning for ourselves. What really matters is helping others win, too, even if it means slowing down and changing our course now and then.

174.

There isn't any one of us who hasn't
felt the loss of someone who's
"way beyond our sight."
From childhood on, we human
beings know the pain of separation
as well as the joy of reunion.
There is something so comforting
to realize that life goes on one way
or another—even when those
we love are way beyond our sight.

175.

Our world hangs like a magnificent
jewel in the vastness of space.
Every one of us is a part of this jewel;
and, in the perspective of infinity,
our differences are infinitesimal.
We are intimately related. May we never
even pretend that we are not.

176.

Finding out that we are one of a kind
could be a lonely and frightening thing
without the reassurance of knowing
that we belong to humankind, and that
all humans laugh and cry about many
of the same things; that all have similar
hopes and fears; that all have many
of the same needs; and that those
needs are best met by other human
beings who can love us for both our
similarities and our differences.

177.

Every human being has value.
This is the basis of all healthy
relationships. Through living
each day as it is given to me,
I've learned that. It cannot be
"taught," but it can be "caught"
from those who live their lives
right along with us.

178.

"What am I really like?
I'm a person who has known
the pain, the joy, the anger,
the sadness, the exhilaration,
and the losses of growing up—
and all the emotions involved in
trying to help my sons grow up.
I translate as much of that as
I know how to into my work."

179.

When I was in college, I went to New York to talk to a songwriter I admired very much. I took him four or five songs that I had written and I thought he'd introduce me to Tin Pan Alley and it would be the beginning of my career. After I played him my songs, he said, "You have very nice songs. Come back when you have a barrelful."

A barrelful of songs! That would mean hundreds of songs. I can still remember the disappointment I felt as I traveled all the way back to college. Nevertheless, that man's counsel was more inspired than I realized. It took me years to understand that. But, of course, what he knew was that if I really wanted to be a songwriter, I'd have to write songs, not just think about the five I had written. And so, after the initial disappointment, I got to work; and through the years, one by one, I have written a barrelful.

In fact, the barrel's overflowing now, and I can tell you, the more I wrote, the better the songs became, and the more those songs expressed what was real within me.

180.

What a *privilege* to be
able to look for the *good*
in our *neighbor*!

181.

We are the holders of a priceless gift,
a gift we received from countless
generations we never knew, a gift that
only we now possess and only we can
give to our children. That unique
gift, of course, is the gift of ourselves.
Whatever we can do to give that
gift, and to help others receive it,
is worth the challenge of all
our human endeavors.

182.

The roots of all our lives go very,
very deep, and we can't really
understand a person unless we have
the chance of knowing who that
person has been, and what
that person has done and liked
and suffered and believed.

183.

The purpose of life is to listen—
to yourself, to your neighbor,
to your world, and to God and,
when the time comes, to respond in
as helpful a way as you can find . . .
from within and without.

184.

How our words
are *understood* doesn't
depend just on how we
express our ideas.
It also depends on how
someone *receives*
what we're saying.

185.

None of us is exactly like anyone else,
but one thing we have in common
is our humanity, our very natural,
understandable desire to know that
at least somebody, onebody, thinks
there's something special about us,
something worth caring about.

186.

The love and interdependence
of parents and children is
universal, and so are the many
difficulties parents and children
have in becoming separate
from one another.

187.

"As we grow, we laugh and cry at many of the same things, and fear many of the same things. At the end, we all leave the same way—by death."

188.

That kind of solitude goes by many names. It may be called "meditation" or "deep relaxation," "quiet time" or "downtime." In some circles, it may even be criticized as "daydreaming." Whatever it's called, it's a time away from outside stimulation, during which inner turbulence can settle, and we have a chance to become more familiar with ourselves.

189.

Being *kind* means *responding*
to the *needs* of others—
and people can be kind,
no matter how old or
how young they are.

190.

It's tempting to think "a little" isn't
significant and that only "a lot" matters.
But most things that are important
in life start very small and change
very slowly, and they don't come
with fanfare and bright lights.

191.

To me, what makes someone successful is managing a healthy combination of wishing and doing. Wishing doesn't make anything happen, but it certainly can be the start of some important happenings.

192.

I hope you'll feel good enough
about yourself, your yesterdays
and your today, that you'll continue
to wish and dream all you can.
And that you'll do all you can to help
the best of your wishes come true.

193.

As different as we are from
one another, as unique as each
one of us is, we are much more
the same than we are different.
That may be the most essential
message of all, as we help
our children grow toward
being caring, compassionate,
and charitable adults.

194.

"I've realized that *everything* does not have to be *perfect* in order to be *effective*."

195.

There is an inner rhythm which sets
the normal beat for human growth.
We need to respect that rhythm in
ourselves, our friends, and in the
children with whom we live and work.
Healthy babies grow from one phase
to another in a predictable way. Human
beings have to learn to crawl before they
learn to walk. And when we're ready to
crawl, we'll find every chance we can to
crawl and crawl and crawl—and we don't
want people to stop us from crawling, and
we don't want people to hurry us to walk.

196.

When we study how our
ancestors dealt with challenges,
we can (hopefully) learn from their
successes and failures, and fashion
our responses to challenges in even
more naturally human ways.

197.

I like to swim, but there are some days
I just don't feel much like doing it—
but I do it anyway! I know it's good
for me and I promised myself I'd do
it every day, and I like to keep my
promises. That's one of my disciplines.
And it's a good feeling after you've
tried and done something well.
Inside you think, "I've kept at this
and I've really learned it—not by
magic, but by my own work."

198.

Most of us, I believe, admire strength.
It's something we tend to respect in
others, desire for ourselves, and wish
for our children. Sometimes, though,
I wonder if we confuse strength with
other words—like aggression and even
violence. Real strength is neither
male nor female; but it is, quite simply,
one of the finest characteristics that
any human being can possess.

199.

When I was a boy I used to think
that strong meant having
big muscles, great physical power;
but the longer I live, the more
I realize that real strength has much
more to do with what is not seen.
Real strength has to do
with helping others.

200.

We speak with more than
our mouths.
We listen with more than
our ears.

201.

I'm proud of you
for all the wishing
and doing that has
helped you get to this
point in your lives, and
I hope you are, too.

202.

I remember one of my seminary professors saying people who were able to appreciate others—who looked for what was good and healthy and kind—were about as close as you could get to God—to the eternal good. And those people who were always looking for what was *bad* about themselves and others were really on the side of evil.

"That's what evil wants," he would say. "Evil wants us to feel so terrible about who we are and who we know, that we'll look with condemning eyes on anybody who happens to be with us at the moment."

203.

"So in loving
and appreciating
our neighbor,
we're participating
in something sacred."

204.

More than 1,500 years ago,
the Roman philosopher Boethius
wrote this sentence:
"Oh happy race of mortals
if your hearts are ruled,
as is the universe, by love."

205.

I encourage you to look
for the good where you are
and embrace it.

206.

We all know people who have grown up to dislike other people who are different—because they are different. I've often noticed that when someone feels that way, that person doesn't feel very good about his or her own differences.

207.

One of the greatest *dignities* of humankind is that each successive generation is invested in the *welfare* of each new generation.

208.

There's a *longing* that
everyone shares . . . and
that is the longing to have
something to give that is
acceptable to others.

209.

I know how important it is to give up our expectations of perfection in any arena of our lives. I know I've tried hard; and yet, every once in a while, I'll entertain the old longing: "Maybe if I could make at least one perfect *segment* of a program . . . ," and I find myself in the trap again.

That doesn't mean we can't produce some highly satisfying moments both for ourselves and others, but it's important to give up—maybe daily—the longing to be perfect. Of course, I think we want it so strongly because we reason that if we are perfect (if we do a perfect job), we will be perfectly lovable. What a heavy burden! Thank God we don't have to *earn* every bit of love that comes our way.

210.

When I think of Robert Frost's poems,
like "The Road Not Taken," I feel
the support of someone who is on
my side, who understands what life's
choices are like, someone who says,
"I've been there, and it's okay to go on."

211.

"There are times all during life when we need the inner resources to keep ourselves busy and productive all by ourselves."

212.

No one of us has
all the answers. . . .
But listening is so important.
Most of us talk a lot and that
doesn't leave much time
for listening.

213.

Childhood isn't just something we
"get through." It's a big journey,
and it's one we've all taken.
Most likely, though, we've
forgotten how much we had
to learn along the way about
ourselves and others.

214.

A friend of mine visited a beautiful monastery where a dozen monks—most of them in their 70s and 80s—were living. This is a place which once had a population of sixty active men studying and following a very strict rule of living: praying together seven different times a day, seven days a week. They worked hard, and they were successful.

My friend asked one of the monks why he felt that over the years the community had dwindled from sixty to twelve. And his reply was: "We did everything right, but somewhere in all that living and praying and successful working, we lost the most important thing of all, the thing that was so contagious and attracted people to us: We lost the naked love. Little by little the success replaced the love."

The old monk ended by saying, "Oh, sure, you can have love *and* success, but the love has to remain first—always first: natural, accepting, affirming, inclusive, naked love."

215.

How each one of us
comes to feel about our
individual uniqueness has
a strong *influence* on how
we feel about *everyone's*
uniqueness.

216.

"Feeling good about
ourselves is essential
in our being able
to love others.**"**

217.

I once asked a ten-year-old how he felt about his older brother going off to camp. There were only two boys in that family, and they were competitive and fought a good deal. My young friend said, "It feels great not to have him around . . . but I kind of miss him." I told him I understood how he could feel both ways at the same time. "In fact," I said, "so many people feel two ways about the same thing that our language even has a word for that." I printed the word *ambivalence* on a slip of paper and gave it to him. "That word is ambivalence," I told him. "People often feel ambivalent." His parents told me later that he carried that slip of paper in his pocket for a couple of weeks and that when they'd ask him how he felt about something, his stock answer for a while was, "Oh, ambivalent, I guess." Just knowing that people could feel like that—and that there was even a name for it—seemed to bring him some relief in his struggles with his conflicting feelings.

218.

It can be a big help for any of us to know that our feelings are OK—that there's nothing wrong with having them, and that lots of other people have the same kinds of feelings as well. We'll always have some feelings we're not proud of, and we can certainly be the objects of our own ambivalence.

If we look at our relationships with any of the many, many people in our lives, I believe we'll always find a measure of ambivalence about our parents, brothers and sisters, other relatives, friends, and even ourselves. An ability to accept our ambivalence toward others may be an important ingredient in relationships that are healthy and lasting.

219.

Relationships are like
dances in which people try
to find whatever happens
to be the mutual *rhythm*
in their lives.

220.

Love and success,
always in that order.
It's that simple
and that difficult.

221.

There's an old Italian proverb:
Qui va piano, va sano, va lentano.
That means: "The person who
goes quietly, goes with health
and goes far." Hurrying up
and using a lot of shortcuts
doesn't get us very far at all.

222.

All life events are formative.
All contribute to what we become,
year by year, as we go on growing.
As my friend the poet Kenneth Koch
once said, "You aren't just the age
you are. You are all the ages
you ever have been!"

223.

Caring comes from the Gothic word
kara, which means "to lament."
So caring is not what a powerful
person gives to a weaker one.
Caring is a matter of being there . . .
lamenting right along with
the one who laments.

224.

Love isn't a state of perfect caring.
It is an active noun like struggle.
To love someone is to strive to accept
that person exactly the way
he or she is, right here and now.

225.

The thing I remember best about
successful people I've met all through
the years is their obvious delight
in what they're doing . . . and it seems
to have very little to do with worldly
success. They just love what
they're doing, and they love it
in front of others.

226.

"A person can grow to his or her fullest capacity only in mutually caring relationships with others."

227.

I started to look behind the things
that people did and said;
and little by little, concluded that
Saint-Exupéry was absolutely right
when he wrote in *The Little Prince*:
"What is essential is invisible to
the eyes." So after a lot of sadness,
I began a lifelong search for what is
essential, what it is about my
neighbor that doesn't meet the eye.

228.

I remember after my grandfather's
death, seeing Dad in the hall with
tears streaming down his face.
I don't think I had ever seen him
cry before. I'm glad I did see him.
It helped me know that it was okay
for men to cry. Many years later,
when my father himself died, I cried;
and way down deep I knew
he would have said it was all right.

229.

Have you noticed that
unhurried time by yourself or
with someone you really trust
can be the best setting for your
own personal growth?

230.

Jane Addams, writing about her Twenty Years at Hull House, said, "People did not want to hear about simple things. They wanted to hear about great things—simply told."

231.

Whether we're a preschooler or a young
teen, a graduating college senior or
a retired person, we human beings
all want to know that we're acceptable,
that our being alive somehow makes
a difference in the lives of others.

232.

I think it's so great that people
can be in a relationship with each
other for the now and not bring
a whole lot of baggage from
their past and a whole lot of
anxiety about the future
to the present moment.

233.

Forgiving and forgetting are often
paired together, but the one certainly
doesn't necessarily follow the other.
Some injuries, real or imagined,
we may never be able to forget, even
though we say we've forgiven them.
Other injuries we may never even
be able to say that we forgive.
Those are the ones, it seems to me,
most likely to involve people we've
loved, and so I'm inclined to
look at what our experiences of
forgiveness may have been like from
the first people who loved us.

234.

One of my wise teachers,
Dr. William F. Orr, told me,
"There is only one thing evil cannot
stand and that is forgiveness."

235.

All we're ever asked to do in
this life is to treat our neighbor—
especially our neighbor who is
in need—exactly as we would
hope to be treated ourselves.
That's our ultimate responsibility.

236.

The older I get, the more I come
to understand that the things
we possess can never bring us
ultimate happiness. Contrary to
what's implied in commercials,
nothing we buy can ever take away
our loneliness or fill our emptiness
or heal our brokenness.

237.

There is a close relationship
between truth and trust.

238.

I believe it's a fact of life that what
we have is less important than what
we make out of what we have.
The same holds true for families:
It's not how many people there
are in a family that counts, but
rather the feelings among
the people who are there.

239.

It isn't only famous movie stars
who want to be alone.
Whenever I hear someone speak of
privacy, I find myself thinking
once again how real and deep
the need for such times is for all
human beings . . . at all ages.

240.

You know yourself—way down
deep—that what really matters
is how we live this life with
our neighbors (those who we
happen to be with at the moment).
That's what really matters.
That's really *all* that matters.

241.

Life is marked by failures
and setbacks and slip-ups, as much
as by hard-won satisfactions
and sudden discoveries of
unexpected strength.
Life is made up of *striving* much
more than attaining.

242.

Yes, Gandhi's one of my heroes . . . Gandhi and Albert Schweitzer and Jane Addams (that tireless advocate of internationalism and world peace), and Bo Lozoff (who helps inmates use their time well in prison). Other heroes are Yo-Yo Ma and everyone else in the public eye who cares about beauty and refuses to bow to fast and loud sensationalism and greed. Recently I've added an "unknown hero" to my list: the person who drives the car I saw the other day, the parked car with the flashing lights and the sign that reads, "Vintage Volunteer . . . Home Delivered Meals."

So those are some of my heroes now. They're the kind of people who help all of us come to realize that "biggest" doesn't necessarily mean "best," that the most important things of life are inside things like feelings and wonder and love—and that the ultimate happiness is being able sometimes, somehow to help our neighbor become a hero too.

243.

I find out more and more
every day how important
it is for people to
share their memories.

244.

I must be an emotional archaeologist
because I keep looking for the
roots of things, particularly the roots
of behavior and why I feel certain ways
about certain things.

245.

If you could only sense how
important you are to the lives
of those you meet;
how important you can be
to the people you may
never even dream of.

246.

Where would any of us be without
teachers—without people
who have passion for their art
or their science or their craft
and love it right in front of us?
What would any of us do without
teachers passing on to us what they
know is essential about life?

247.

The urge to make and build
seems to be an almost universal
human characteristic.
It goes way beyond meeting our
need for survival and seems to be
the expression of some deep-rooted
part of being human.

248.

There is something of yourself
that you leave at every meeting
with another person.

249.

From the song
I Did Too

Did you ever fall and hurt your hand or knee?
Did you ever bite your tongue?
Did you ever find the stinger of a bee
Stuck in your thumb?
Did you ever trip and fall down on the stairs?
Did you ever stub your toe?
Did you ever dream of great big grizzly bears
Who wouldn't go?
I did too.
It seems the things that you do,
I did too when I was very new.
I had lots of hurts and scares and worries
When I was growing up like you.

250.

Finding the inner readiness to do new things is such an important part of growth. It's one of those things that can be encouraged and supported, but can't be hurried. A berry ripens in its own good time . . .

251.

There are three ways
to ultimate success:
The first way is to be kind.
The second way is to be kind.
The third way is to be kind.

252.

Have you noticed how delighted young children are to hear their parents tell stories of things they did when they were little? Part of that delight comes from shared moments of closeness with a person you love, and part of it comes from hearing that someone you love had the same kinds of feelings you now have, did some of the same things, got dirty, got in trouble, laughed and cried and felt afraid.

253.

I don't think anyone
can *grow* unless he's
loved exactly as he is *now*,
appreciated for what
he *is* rather than
what he *will* be.

254.

I'm *proud* of you
for the *times* you came
in second, or third, or fourth,
but what you *did* was
the *best* you had ever done.

255.

You don't ever have to do anything
sensational for people to love you.
When I say, "It's you I like,"
I'm talking about that part of you
that knows that life is far more than
anything you can ever see or hear
or touch . . . that deep part of you that
allows you to stand for those things
without which humankind cannot
survive: love that conquers hate,
peace that rises triumphant over war,
and justice that proves more
powerful than greed.

256.

In every neighborhood,
all across our country,
there are good people
insisting on a good start
for the young, and doing
something about it.

257.

"The receiving in life to me is one of the greatest gifts that we give another person. And it's very hard. Because when you give, you're in much greater control. But when you receive something— you're vulnerable."

258.

From the song
The Clown in Me

Sometimes I feel when I'm afraid
That I will never make the grade
So I pretend I'm someone else
And show the world my other self.
I'm not quite sure of me, you see
When I have to make a clown of me.
A clown, a clown
I think I'll be a clown.
I think I'll make the people laugh
And laugh all over town. A clown,
That's what I'll be, a clown.
Sometimes I feel all the good inside
And haven't got a thing to hide.
My friends all tell me I'm the best;
They think I'm better than the rest.

It's times like this I act myself
And I let the clown stay on the shelf.
Myself, myself
I think I'll be myself.
I think I'll let the people see
The comfortable inside of me.
Myself, I'll be myself.
It's only when I feel let down
I might be scared into a clown.
But he can be himself
When I can be myself, myself.
I think I'll be myself.

259.

Honesty is often very hard.
The truth is often painful.
But the freedom it can bring
is worth the trying.

260.

The values we care about the deepest,
and the movements within society
that support those values, command
our love. When those things that
we care about so deeply become
endangered, we become enraged.
And what a healthy thing that is!
Without it, we would never stand up
and speak out for what we believe.

261.

It's the people we love the most
who can make us feel
the gladdest . . . and the maddest!
Love and anger are such a puzzle!

262.

The toughest thing is to love
somebody who has done
something mean to you—
especially when that somebody
is yourself. Look inside yourself
and find that loving part of you.
Take good care of that part because
it helps you love your neighbor.

263.

Each generation, in its turn,
is a link between all that has gone
before and all that comes after.
That is true genetically,
and it is equally true in
the transmission of identity.

264.

"It came to me ever so slowly
that the best way to know
the truth was to begin
trusting what my inner truth
was . . . and trying to
share it—not right away—
only after I had worked hard
at trying to understand it."

265.

The best thing a person can feel
is to be accepted as he is,
not as he will be when
he grows up, but as he is now,
right this very minute.

266.

It's hard for us, as adults, to understand
and manage our angry feelings
toward parents, spouses, and children,
or to keep their anger toward us
in perspective. It's a different kind
of anger from the kind we may
feel toward strangers because it is
so deeply intertwined with
caring and attachment.

267.

We don't have to understand all
of someone else's creative efforts.
What's important is that we
communicate our respect
for their attempts to express
what's inside themselves.

268.

"Love and trust, in the space
between what's said
and what's heard in
our life, can make all the
difference in this world."

269.

The outside things of life certainly
do change and often quickly, but the
inside things remain. Our parents
and their parents and their parents—
all of us—were created by Love.
Love with a capital L.
And we spend our lives trying
to recognize that we truly *are*
lovable and capable of loving.

270.

We all have our limits of patience and endurance, no matter what age we are, and that's something children need to know is natural, human, and acceptable.

271.

" Helping has two sides—asking
for help and giving help.
Whether we're young or old,
helping can enrich both
the receiver and the giver. "

272.

We're all on a journey—each one of us.
And if we can be sensitive to the person
who happens to be our "neighbor,"
that, to me, is the greatest challenge
as well as the greatest pleasure.
Because if you're trusted, then
people will allow you to share their
inner garden—what greater gift!

273.

Competition. It's a word that makes many of us very edgy, and it's a situation that we have probably been living with since we were very small.

For some people competition is a thrill, a stimulation, a challenge. For others, it's a source of sadness and anger and apprehension. For still others, it's a mixture of all those things.

It's not possible to go through life without competing. As one woman told me, "Competition is a part of our everyday life, whether we're competing for a job, or on the soccer field, or for love."

There are many kinds of competition, to be sure. But I think that love does have something to do with them all. In fact, I believe that if we've ever wanted someone's love, then we've known what competition really means.

274.

Deep within us—no matter who
we are—there lives a feeling of
wanting to be lovable, of wanting
to be the kind of person that others
like to be with. And the greatest thing
we can do is to let people know that
they are loved and capable of loving.

275.

The first time we required forgiveness, we probably did something we shouldn't have when our closest grown-ups thought we should have known better. We made someone angry. We were to blame. What did the first brush with blame begin to teach us?

If we were fortunate, we began to learn that "to err is human." . . . The second thing we learned (if we were fortunate) was that having someone we loved get mad at us did not mean that person had stopped loving us; we had their unconditional love, and that meant we would have their forgiveness, too.

276.

I am glad that I've been able to do
what I've done and not been
sidetracked along the way.
A teacher of mine calls it
guided drift. Isn't that wonderful?
You're drifting, and yet
you've got a rudder.

277.

We all need to *learn* that
life is a mixture of what
is and is *not* possible.

278.

Sometimes it surprises me
to think that my work on
that first children's program
was almost by chance!
Isn't it mysterious how so
many wonderful things in life
come to us seemingly
without our planning?

279.

Transitions are almost always
signs of growth, but they
can bring feelings of loss.
To get somewhere new,
we may have to leave
somewhere else behind.

280.

I saw a friend who's a freelance writer and asked him what he was working on. "Nothing right now," he answered. "You know how it is for freelancers. But at times like this I tell myself I'm 'between opportunities.' That way I don't have to feel I'm nowhere."

There's often a tendency for us to hurry through transitions. We may feel that these transitions are "nowhere at all" compared to what's gone before or what we anticipate is next to come. But you are somewhere . . . you're "between."

281.

The really important "great" things
are never center stage of life's dramas;
they're always "in the wings."
That's why it's so essential for us
to be mindful of the humble
and the deep rather than
the flashy and the superficial.

282.

It can sometimes be difficult to *ask*
for support when we need it,
but having *someone* we can
count on to stick with us through
the tough times can make those
times much more *bearable*.

283.

As work grows out of play,
an attitude toward work grows
with it—an attitude that may persist
all through our workaday life.
That attitude can have a lot to do
with how we accept challenges,
how we can cope with failures,
and whether we can find the inner
fulfillment that makes working,
in and of itself, worthwhile.

284.

Every human being needs
to be *loved* and needs to be able
to love in *return*.
That is what allows us
to be *human*.

285.

The more I think about it, the more
I wonder if God and neighbor are
somehow One. "Loving God,
Loving neighbor"—the same thing?
For me, coming to recognize that
God loves every neighbor is
the ultimate appreciation!

286.

Often when you think you're at the end
of something, you're at the beginning
of something else. I've felt that many
times. My hope for all of us is that
"the miles we go before we sleep"
will be filled with all the feelings that
come from deep caring—delight,
sadness, joy, wisdom—and that in
all the endings of our life, we will be
able to see the new beginnings.

287.

The great poet
Rainer Maria Rilke wrote:
"Be patient towards all that
is unsolved in your heart,
and learn to love
the questions themselves."

288.

Whether the other be an adult
or a child, our engagement in listening
to who that person is can often be
our greatest gift. Whether that person
is speaking or playing or dancing,
building or singing or painting,
if we care, we can listen.

289.

One summer, midway through Seminary, I was on a weekend vacation in a little town in New England. I decided on Sunday to go hear a visiting preacher in the little town's chapel. I heard the worst sermon I could have ever imagined. I sat in the pew thinking, "He's going against every rule they're teaching us about preaching. What a waste of time!" That's what I thought until the very end of the sermon when I happened to see the person beside me with tears in her eyes whispering, "He said exactly what I needed to hear." It was then that I knew something very important had happened in that service. The woman beside me had come in need. Somehow the words of that poorly crafted sermon had been translated into a message that spoke to her heart. On the other hand, I had come in judgment, and I heard nothing but the faults.

It was a long time before I realized it, but that sermon's effect on the person beside me turned out to be one of the great lessons of my life. Thanks to that preacher and listener-in-need, I now know that the space between a person doing his or her best to deliver a message of good news and the needy listener is holy ground. Recognizing that seems to have allowed me to forgive myself for being the accuser that day. In fact, that New England Sunday experience has fueled my desire to be a better advocate, a better "neighbor," wherever I am.

290.

One of the most *essential* ways
of saying "I love you" is
being a *receptive* listener.

291.

A friend of mine was in a taxi in
Washington, D.C., going slowly past
the National Archives, when he noticed
the words on the cornerstone of the
building: "The past is prologue."
He read them out loud to the taxi driver
and said, "What do you think that
means, 'The past is prologue'?"
The taxi driver said, "I think it means,
'Man, you ain't seen nothin' yet!'"

292.

Have you ever worked as hard as you knew how and people still didn't appreciate you? What do you do? You either give up or you keep on.

What will you do about your hard times? I wonder what is in store for you and what you will make of it. What kind of opportunities will you have to use the talents you've been given? Who will help you? How will you respond to your successes? How will you help the children in your life to grow and develop into confident, helpful adults? How will you respond to people with obvious disabilities? Will you use your own disability (we all have them, you know) to understand or to separate you from your neighbor? What kind of person are you going to be?

293.

I recently learned that in an average
lifetime a person walks about
sixty-five thousand miles.
That's two and a half times around
the world. I wonder where your steps
will take you. I wonder how you'll use
the rest of the miles you're given.

294.

Even if it were possible to give
someone everything he or she
asked for, we would be depriving
that person of many ways of
growing. We all need to learn
that life is a mixture of what
is and is not possible.

295.

Sometimes it takes years and years of experimentation to realize who we can be . . . what we can make of what has come to us. No one would have ever predicted that Mahatma Gandhi would become the person to dramatically change the life of people in India. He even went to England when he was young to explore whether it might be better to be an Englishman. But look how he put it all together later on.

Maybe it's happened to you already when you can actually integrate what you've learned with your own personality—when you can actually use your education to be who you want to be, to choose out of that mixed bag of explorations what you want to call yourself. That's when your education adds an extra measure of excitement!

296.

"Adults don't have to be
perfect to be acceptable.
People of every age
need to know that."

297.

There are all kinds of *artists* in the world. If people can combine the talent that they have *inside* of them with the hard work that it takes to *develop* it, they can become *true* artists.

298.

My hunch is that the beginning of
my belief in the caring nature of God
came from all of those people—
all of those extraordinary, ordinary
people who believed that I was more
than I thought I was—all those saints
who helped a shy kid to see more
clearly what was really essential.

299.

As work grows out of play,
an attitude toward work grows
with it—an attitude that may
persist through our workaday life.
That attitude can have a lot to do
with how we accept challenges,
how we cope with failures, and
whether we can find in the jobs we do,
the inner fulfillment that makes
working worthwhile, in and of itself.

300.

When we know care is there,
life can seem well worth living,
even with the ups and downs
of our ever-changing world.

301.

When I was very young, most of
my childhood heroes wore capes,
flew through the air, or picked up
buildings with one arm.
They were spectacular and got a lot
of attention. But as I grew, my heroes
changed, so that now I can honestly
say that anyone who does anything
to help a child is a hero to me.

302.

I wrote in a song that in the long,
long trip of growing, there are stops
along the way. It's important to
know when we need to stop, reflect,
and receive. In our competitive
world, that might be called
a waste of time. I've learned that
those times can be the preamble to
periods of enormous growth.

303.

Even good people sometimes do
bad things. Errors might mean
corrections, apologies, repairs,
but they didn't mean that we,
as a person, were a bad person
in the sight of those we loved.

304.

In 1963, President John F. Kennedy went
to Dallas, Texas. He was going to speak
there. If he had lived, these are some
of the words that he had written to say:
"We ask that we may be worthy of our
power and responsibility—that we may
exercise our strength with wisdom."
It's hard work to exercise our strength
with wisdom, to be responsible stewards
of what we've been given. You know how
hard it is. You can't satisfy all the desires
of those who ask, but you can translate
some of the care you have inside of
yourself to action on the outside.

305.

Teilhard de Chardin, a 19th century
philosopher, writes that someone
scrawled the following words on
the bulletin board of the great
Notre-Dame Cathedral:
"Le monde demain appartiendra
à ceux qui lui ont apporté
la plus grande espérance."
The world tomorrow will belong
to those who brought it
the greatest hope.

306.

Most of us have so few moments of quiet
in our lives. There's noise everywhere.
There are some places we can't even escape
it. Television and radio are probably the
worst culprits. They are very seductive.
It's so tempting for some people to turn
on the television set or the radio when they
first walk into a room or get in the car . . .
to fill any space with noise. I wonder what
some people are afraid might happen
in the silence. Some of us must have
forgotten how nourishing silence can be.

307.

There is much more to independence
than learning to master new skills.
One of the most important parts of
independence is learning to form
new relationships with other people.

308.

I feel I've been greatly blessed by
many people I've been able to meet and
come to know. Sure, I've worked hard.
You don't choose a job and expect
not to work hard. But you can expect
that you don't have to do it alone.
Nobody should have to do it alone.

309.

There are times when
explanations, no matter
how reasonable,
just don't seem to help.

310.

When I think of solitude, I think of an anecdote from *With the Door Open: My Experience* by the late Danish religious philosopher Johannes Anker Larsen: "The most comprehensive formula for human culture which I know was given by the old peasant who, on his death bed, obtained from his son this one promise: to sit every day for half an hour alone in the best room."

311.

"Each of our life journeys is unique. No child will take the same journey as the parent, and no parent can determine what a child's journey will be."

312.

It may be that the most important mastery we achieve early on is not the mastery of a particular skill or particular piece of knowledge, but rather the mastery of the patience and persistence that learning requires, along with the ability to expect and accept mistakes and the feelings of disappointment they may bring.

313.

Human *relationships* are *primary* in all of living.

314.

I enjoy working on our program, but, of course, as with any kind of work, we have some frustrating times. Often those are when we have problems with the equipment when we're taping in the studio. It can also be frustrating when I am trying to write something and can't seem to get an idea that feels right. Sometimes, when I'm working on a script or composing a song, writing flows easily, but there are lots of times it doesn't. It's probably true that all writers have frustrating and discouraging moments.

Sometimes it helps me to get away from the work—by taking a walk, sitting in a quiet room, listening to music, talking with a friend.

315.

Beside my chair is a saying in French.
It inspires me every day. It's a sentence
from Saint-Exupéry's *The Little Prince*,
and it reads, *"L'essentiel est invisible
pour les yeux."* (What is essential
is invisible to the eyes.)
The closer we get to know the
truth of that sentence, the closer
I feel we get to wisdom.

316.

Even people who care
deeply about each other
can agree to disagree
about some things.

317.

When I was a boy and I would see
scary things in the news, my mother
would say to me, "Look for the helpers.
You will always find people who
are helping." To this day, especially
in times of "disaster," I remember
my mother's words, and I am always
comforted by realizing that there
are still so many helpers—so many
caring people in this world.

318.

We want to raise our
children so that they can
take a sense of pleasure
in both their own heritage
and the diversity of others.

319.

When we study how our ancestors dealt with challenges, we can (hopefully) learn from their successes *and* failures.

Someone once asked Edison if he was disappointed after trying 382 ways of making a lightbulb. He answered that he wasn't. He was glad that he now knew 382 ways *not* to try.

320.

That which has real value in life in
any millennium is very simple.
Very deep and very simple! It happens
inside of us—in the "essential invisible"
part of us, and that is what allows
everyone to be a potential neighbor.

321.

We need to help people to discover
the true meaning of love.
Love is generally confused with
dependence. Those of us who have
grown in true love know that
we can love only in proportion to
our capacity for independence.

322.

Children who have learned to be
comfortably dependent can become
not only comfortably independent,
but can also become comfortable
with having people depend on them.
They can lean, or stand and be leaned
upon, because they know what a good
feeling it can be to feel needed.

323.

The media shows the tiniest percentage
of what people do. There are millions
and millions of people doing
wonderful things all over the world,
and they're generally not
the ones being touted in the news.

324.

When we love a person, we accept
him or her exactly as is: the lovely
with the unlovely, the strong along
with the fearful, the true mixed in
with the facade, and of course,
the only way we can do it is by
accepting ourselves that way.

325.

That's the way true neighborliness grows— loving others as we first loved ourselves.

326.

One of the most essential ways
of saying, "I love you" is by
careful listening—listening
with "the ear of the heart."

327.

From the song
Please Don't Think It's Funny

In the long, long trip of growing,
There are stops along the way
For thoughts of all the soft things
And a look at yesterday.
For a chance to fill our feelings
With comfort and with ease,
And then tell the new tomorrow:
"You can come now when you please."

328.

We don't have to think it's funny when
we feel like we need some extra comfort.
I sometimes sing about that to children,
but, as you know, I believe there's
a child somewhere in each of us.
We all have times like that—
times when an extra measure of
care is needed. We need comfort
and so does everyone else.
And it's nothing to be ashamed of.

329.

A friend dreamed of going to medical school when he was young. Growing up, he worked in his father's small auto-repair shop, but he knew that one day he was going to be a doctor. That dream never came true. When he was finishing high school, his father had a heart attack, and my friend took over the business to support the family.

"Sure I'd like to have been a doctor," he says, "but what's a person to do? It was tough to let go of that dream, but I've found a lot of satisfaction in my work, even though I didn't think life would work out this way."

330.

Recently, I declared a day to be alone
with myself. I took a long drive and
played a tape. When I got to the
mountains, I read and prayed
and listened and slept. In fact, I can't
remember having a calmer sleep in
a long, long time. The next day I went
back to work and did more than
I usually get done in three days.

331.

Imagining something may be
the first step in making it happen,
but it takes the real time and real
efforts of real people to learn things,
make things, turn thoughts into
deeds or visions into inventions.

332.

When I was ordained, it was for
a special ministry, that of serving
children and families through
television. I consider that what I do
through *Mister Rogers' Neighborhood*
is my ministry. A ministry doesn't
have to be only through a church,
or even through an ordination.
And I think we all can minister
to others in this world by being
compassionate and caring.

333.

All through our lives there are resignations of wishes. As children, once we learn to walk, we must resign ourselves to not being a baby anymore. If we just want to be taken care of and not make any effort to do more and more for ourselves, then we can avoid that resignation and just stay a baby.

You may know some adults who are still babies. Even though they're mentally and physically able people, they still want to be served all the time. How sad for them, not to have been able to experience the excitement of growing from one part of life to another.

334.

"Love is like infinity: You can't have more or less infinity, and you can't compare two things to see if they're 'equally infinite.' Infinity just is, and that's the way I think love is, too."

335.

You bring *all* you ever were
and are to any *relationship*
you have *today*.

336.

One evening, as I sat at the piano, I began to play a song—almost without thinking. Little by little, the words came to me, and I realized it was a song I had known for many years about all our wishes coming true. It was called, "When You Wish Upon a Star." I remember when I was a boy and first heard that song, I had such a wonderful feeling. To think that wishing could make things come true was such a splendid idea to me. And I had lots of wishes.

But, years later, playing that song and thinking those words, it dawned on me how important it was that all my wishes had *not* come true; of course, it was equally important that some of them actually had. And I wondered about the difference.

"When you wish upon a star . . ." Why, there are whole galaxies that we haven't even discovered yet, stars way out in space and stars within ourselves that are patiently waiting to be hitched to the work of our lives to brighten up our world.

I don't know your wishes or your hopes. Nobody but you and the people you care to share them with should know them. Wishes are sometimes grand and far beyond the reality of the present, but other wishes are intimate. They are about simple things . . . simple private things.

I trust that you'll feel good enough about yourself to do all you can to help the best of your wishes come true.

337.

There would be no art, and there would be no science, if human beings had no desire to create. And if we had everything we ever needed or wanted, we would have no reason for creating anything. So, at the root of all art and all science there exists a gap— a gap between what the world is like and what we wish and hope for it to be like. Our unique way of bridging that gap in each of our lives seems to me to be the essence of the reason for human creativity.

338.

Try your best to make
goodness attractive.
That's one of the toughest
assignments you'll
ever be given.

339.

I often think of what Will Durant wrote in *The Story of Civilization*: "Civilization is a stream with banks. The stream is sometimes filled with blood from people killing, stealing, shouting, and doing things historians usually record—while, on the banks, unnoticed, people build homes, make love, raise children, sing songs, write poetry, whittle statues. The story of civilization is the story of what happens on the banks."

340.

I hope you're proud of yourself
for the times you've said "yes,"
when all it meant was extra work
for you and was seemingly helpful
only to somebody else.

341.

We don't always *succeed*
in what we try—certainly
not by the world's standards—
but I think you'll find it's
the willingness to *keep trying*
that matters most.

342.

What makes the difference between
wishing and realizing our wishes?
Lots of things, of course, but the main
one, I think, is whether we link our
wishes to our active work. It may take
months or years, but it's far more likely
to happen when we care so much that
we'll work as hard as we can to make
it happen. And when we're working
toward the realization of our wishes,
some of our greatest strengths
come from the encouragement of
people who care about us.

343.

Helen Ross was a good friend who taught teachers, doctors, and psychiatrists and consulted with professionals working with children and families all over the world. She was one of the great people of our age in the understanding of the dynamic development of human beings. After one operation for cancer and some subsequent therapy, Helen chose to refuse treatment when her cancer reappeared. One day when I visited her, I found Helen very frail, yet interested in all that I had to tell her about our television work and her Pittsburgh friends. Some of the time I just held her hand and we said nothing. We didn't have to.

After one of those silences, Helen said to me, "Do you ever pray for people, Fred?"

"Of course I do." So I said, "Dear God, encircle us with Thy love wherever we may be."

And Helen replied, "That's what it is, isn't it?—it's love. That's what it's all about."

Helen was eighty-eight when she died. She had spent most of her adult life working at understanding the complexities of human growth and development, and her summation of life was that love is what it's all about.

344.

The most important moments are rarely in the bright lights with cameras rolling and mikes recording. The most important moments are rarely center stage; they most often happen "in the wings."

Have you found that to be true, too? That what you expected to be the big occasion or the main event turned out to be merely an excuse for you to be somewhere in order to be touched by something you might have otherwise considered of little importance?

345.

It is tempting to cling to the familiar.
Just like in music, if we keep living . . .
playing in the key of C, we wouldn't
have to take any risks of not making it
to the key of E-flat. But we'd never
know what it sounded like unless
we tried. And once we've had
the practice and the pleasure
of making a transition from one key
to the next, the subsequent times
might not be quite so difficult.

346.

You can't be a winner
all the time.

347.

In the external scheme of things,
shining moments are as brief as
the twinkling of an eye, yet such
twinklings are what eternity is
made of—moments when we
human beings can say "I love you,"
"I'm proud of you," "I forgive you,"
"I'm grateful for you."
That's what eternity is made of:
invisible, imperishable good stuff.

348.

I trust as time goes on, you will be aware deep inside yourself of the kind of difference you have been privileged to make.

349.

"No matter what our age,
no matter what our condition,
life's disappointments often
show us the limits of what we're
able to do. But, of course,
in dealing with them,
we just might create
a new forward striving."

350.

From the song
**What Do You Do With
the Mad You Feel**

What do you do with the mad that you feel
When you feel so mad you could bite?
When the whole wide world
Seems oh, so wrong
And nothing you do seems very right?
What do you do? Do you punch a bag?
Do you pound some clay or some dough?
Do you round up friends for a game of tag?
Or see how fast you go?
It's great to be able to stop
When you've planned a thing that's wrong.
And be able to do something else instead
And think this song:

I can stop when I want to,
Can stop when I wish.
Can stop, stop, stop anytime.
And what a good feeling to feel like this,
And know that the feeling is really mine.
Know that there's something deep inside
That helps us become what we can,
For a girl can be someday a woman
And a boy can be someday a man.

351.

"Play does seem to open up another part of the mind that is always there, but that, since childhood, may have become closed off and hard to reach. When we treat children's play as seriously as it deserves, we are helping them feel the joy that's to be found in the creative spirit. We're helping ourselves stay in touch with that spirit, too."

352.

When we're taking risks at any time
in our lives, trying new things,
whether it's a new job, or a diet,
or a different lifestyle, it certainly helps
to know that people who love us will urge
us to keep trying, and will also offer
a hand, an ear, or even a shoulder to cry
on when we feel like giving up.
Maybe, too, they'll help us remember,
even as we're disappointed about
what we can't do, that there is
much we *can* do.

353.

When the gusty winds
blow and shake our *lives*,
if we know that there are
those people who *care* about us,
we may *bend* with the wind—
but we won't *break*.

354.

From the song
I'm Proud of You

I'm proud of you. I'm proud of you.
I hope that you're as proud as I am.
And that you're
Learning how important you are,
How important each person you see can be.
Discovering each one's specialty
Is the most important learning.
I'm proud of you. I'm proud of you.
I hope that you are proud of you, too!

355.

Little by little we human
beings are confronted
with situations that give us
more and more clues
that we aren't perfect.

356.

I'm proud of you for the times you've said, "No," when all it seemed to mean was a loss of pleasure, yet eventually supported the growth of somebody else and yourself.

I'm proud of you for standing up for something you believed in—something that wasn't particularly popular, but that assured the rights of someone less fortunate than you.

I'm proud of you for anything that allows you to feel proud of yourself.

357.

"The child is in me still . . . and sometimes not so still."

358.

You will be the senators and the doctors and the nurses and the lawyers and the educators and the mothers and the fathers of the next generation, and I trust that you'll have the opportunity to participate fully in this wonderful world of ours. You'll be the ones who will make the decisions. You'll be the ones who will make the difference.

359.

Parents are like shuttles on a loom.
They join the threads of the past
with the threads of the future
and leave their own bright patterns
as they go, providing continuity
to succeeding ages.

360.

May you seek out your own
continuing life education and,
over time, over your whole lifetime,
may you grow in faith and reverence,
uprightness in morals, knowledge
of language and arts, forgiveness,
honesty, commitment, maturity,
and your capacity to love.

361.

"You'll be the one to decide your next steps . . . and the next steps won't all be easy—not by any means—but if they're honest, they'll be worth the try. Any real work has its tough times (you know that), and any real love has its trials."

362.

My hope for you at the beginning
of this new moment in your life
is that you will take good care
of that part of you where your
best dreams come from,
that invisible part of you
that allows you to look on
yourself and your neighbor
with delight.

363.

From Fred Rogers' Speech for the Graduating Class of Latrobe High School, His Alma Mater

"You shall know the truth, and the truth shall make you free."

It's hard for me to believe that it was 1946 when I last sat in this room looking up at those words above this stage. I can tell you, most of my thoughts during my commencement week had to do with plans for the summer or the next year, certainly not fifty years from then! In fact, if somebody had told me that I would go to college and study music and theology and finally produce television programs for young children, I wouldn't have believed them.

For one thing, I thought I was going to be an airline pilot. (I took flying lessons all during my senior year at the Latrobe Airport.) Obviously I didn't make that dream come true. It was as if I was meant to do something I never even thought about. How could I have thought about it? In those days, hardly anybody was thinking about television!

Yet all the while, somewhere inside of me, I carried those words, "The truth shall make you free." And I tried almost unconsciously to discover the truth about who I was and about my neighbor (the person I happened to be with at the moment). I found out, at every turn in the road, that truth seemed to set me free enough to go on.

Dr. Fred Rainsberry was the person who first put me in front of the television camera. For eight years I had co-produced a daily program called *The Children's Corner*. I wrote and played the music and voiced the puppets all behind the set.

When Dr. Rainsberry, the head of children's programming, asked me to work for his department at the Canadian Broadcasting Corporation, he said, "Fred, I've seen you talk with kids. Let's put you yourself on the air." I told him I'd never done such a thing, but he replied, "Let's give it a try. We'll call it 'Mister Rogers.'" His confidence and support launched me into something I may have never dared to do on my own.

Fifty years from now I trust that you'll look back over your journey and recognize the blessings—great and small—which helped to carry you through, and also realize how other people shared their truth and their light with you and made the trip less lonely.

You know, none of us gets to be competent, mature people without the help of others. By now you've discovered that you don't have to go it alone. In fact, no one gets to be a graduate without the investment of other people: people who have loved you all along the way.

During this extra-special time, I'd like to give you a minute to think of those who have believed in you . . . those who have helped you live your life knowing what was good and real.

A minute of silence for all of us to remember those who have cared about us through our lives: people who have made a significant difference in our being who we are right now. One minute of silence.

Whomever you've been thinking about, whether they're here or far away or even in heaven, imagine how pleased they'd be to know that you recognize what a difference they've made in your becoming. And I trust that you'll discover how much our world needs your truth.

364.

From the song
Won't You Be My Neighbor?

I have always wanted to have a neighbor
Just like you!
I've always wanted to live in a
Neighborhood with you.
So let's make the most of this beautiful day;
Since we're together we might as well say,
Would you be mine?
Could you be mine?
Won't you be my neighbor?

365.

So in all that you do
in all of your life, I wish you
the *strength* and the *grace*
to make those *choices*
which will allow you and
your neighbor to become
the *best* of whoever *you* are.

About the Author

Credit: Walt Seng

Known as "America's Favorite Neighbor," Fred Rogers dedicated his life to serving children through public television as creator, composer, and host of *Mister Rogers' Neighborhood*. He studied at the University of Pittsburgh Graduate School of Child Development and was ordained a Presbyterian minister, with the unique charge of working with children and families through television. Fred Rogers' relentless commitment to all that is best in people led to an astonishing array of honors, from induction into the Television Hall of Fame to the Presidential Medal of Freedom. Fred Rogers passed away in February 2003.

Mister Rogers' Neighborhood first debuted in 1968 on PBS and for over forty years has defined television at its finest.